Because of the Storm

Original story:
Jennifer Degenhardt

Translator:
Arina Glozman

Cover artists:
Elysees Lincecum & Dante Hall

For all the immigrant children who arrive in the United States unaccompanied, this story is for you.

table of contents

ACKNOWLEDGEMENTS

I am so grateful for the collaboration with Lisa Funston, artist and owner of Paint It Black Art in Carlsbad, California (@paintitblackartca on Instagram). If you're playing along at home, Lisa is a friend of a friend of my cousin who reached out to me via Instagram and told me about her business teaching art to students. No way! Student artists who may want to draw images for the covers of my books?!? Yes, please!

What usually happens is that I give Lisa a list of titles that need cover art and she asks her students (if they're interested) to choose. Because of the pandemic and a rough 2022, I double booked on artists for this story: hence the different front and back covers.

I am delighted with the artwork from Elysees Lincecum, a Paint It Black Art student, and Dante Hall, a younger artist who is the son of a language teacher colleague, Sara Hall (an author, too). It is always so much fun for me to see what students can create with a simple description of the story, yet without reading the book itself. They do their own research and come up with an idea they think will best represent the story. I think they get it right every time.

Thank you, too, to Jennifer Lighty and Finishing Line Press for the permission to reprint the poem, *Ghost Moon Lullaby*, which is featured at the end of this book, and which was written in response to the situation at the southern border of the United States with respect to the detention of child immigrants. Aside from growing up in the same town and having the same name, Jennifer Lighty and I seem to be creating similar existences through writing. You can read more of her work at https://jenlighty.substack.com/. Thank you, Jennifer, for trusting me once again with your poem (original reprint of the same poem was in 2018 in the Spanish version of this story, *Debido a la tormenta*).

Chapter 1

I am at home. My godmother tells me, "Andrés, I need to go to the market. I'll be back soon."

I don't respond. I don't say anything.

She leaves the house and I'm alone. I'm in the living room with a toy. I play with it and wait for her to come back.

I am 4 years old.

*****

I live with my godmother in San Pedro Sula, Honduras. I have lived here for a long time. My parents aren't here, though. My godmother says that they are in the United States, far from here. I don't understand why.

My godmother is nice, but I want my parents. I want to be with them.

My godmother and I live in a very small house in the city. We don't have a lot of money, but the house does have a phone. My godmother always tells me, "Andrés, don't answer the phone. You're not allowed."

Sometimes the phone rings. My godmother answers. She picks it up and says, "Hello." After a few seconds she speaks again. It's a mystery to me.

One day I ask, "*Madrina¹*, what are you doing?"

"I'm talking with a friend," she tells me. "But you shouldn't touch the phone."

*****

One day when my godmother is at the market, the phone rings.

Nobody is home. I'm alone.

I pick up the phone and say, "Hello?"

There is a person who speaks. The voice says, "Andrés? Is that you?"

---

¹ Madrina: godmother.

"Yes."

It's my mother. I haven't talked to her in a long time.

THE VOICE

Vol. 7 No. 12   Serrano, Arizona   19 March, 2018

Young Migrants: The Push

There are many children and young adults who are leaving their countries in Central America to come to the United States. Sometimes they even travel alone, without family. The reasons for leaving are different in every country, but in the countries of the Northern Triangle (El Salvador, Guatemala, and Honduras), many problems exist which cause the young people to leave.

In all of these countries there are economic problems. But violence is the particular problem in Honduras due to the instability of their political situation. This violence is caused by gangs such as the *Marasalvatrucha* (MS13), and *Calle 18* in El Salvador. These groups make life difficult for everyone, often demanding money for protection. Those groups also use children as the "eyes" of the gangs, watching out for police and other law enforcement.

The situation is desperate. Young people want to leave so they can escape the violence and other problems.

Chapter 2

I have not seen my mother in more than two years. She is away with my father. "They are working," my godmother tells me. And that's why it's necessary for me to live with my godmother.

My godmother is a friend of my parents. She doesn't have children. I live with her while my parents are away in the United States. My father was the one to leave first. A year later my mom left, too.

My godmother wants to keep me with her.

"You are my son," she tells me. But she isn't my mother. I want to be with my real mother.

*****

Today when my godmother is at the market, I talk to my mom on the telephone.

"Andrés. You need to listen to me. If you want to see me again, you need to listen."

It's a miracle that I can even talk with my mother today, so of course I listen to her.

My mother tells me that there is a plan. The plan is that one day one of my aunts will come over to visit me.

My mom tells me, "When your aunt leaves to go home, you need to cry and say that you want to go with her. Her house is in Quebrada Seca, near San Pedro Sula."

*****

The day of the visit arrives. When she goes to the door to leave, I cry, "*Tía*[2], I want to visit my grandfather! I want to go with you!"

I cry a lot. My godmother speaks with my aunt. Finally, my godmother tells me that I can go with her for three days.

*****

Three days become three months. My godmother loves me and comes to Quebrada

---

[2] Tía: aunt.

Seca many times to try to take me back with her, but I don't go.

At four years old, I live with my aunt and grandfather.

Chapter 3

I live in the house with my grandfather and my mother's siblings. They are 12 and 17 years old. There is not a lot of space in the house. I'm doing okay, but I want my mother. I haven't spoken with her for a long time.

One day, I go to live at the house of another aunt. I don't know why. She has a husband and a young child. I don't want to live with them, but I don't have a choice. I am five years old.

I don't like living with this aunt and uncle. The aunt is mean and so is the son. The husband is nice, but he works, so I don't see much of him.

*****

One day everything changes. My aunt is crying and yelling a lot. I don't say anything, but I listen. She uses the words "die" and "dead". My uncle is not alive. He's dead.

After this day, the situation in the house is horrible. My aunt is very sad. She treats me very badly. Her son treats me badly, too. They don't want me, but they want the money.

"Andrés, I don't want you. You live in this house because of the money."

"What money?" I ask. I am six years old, and I don't understand.

"Your parents are paying me money to watch you," she tells me. "But it's not enough."

I think a lot about her words. Everything is horrible.

My aunt goes on "vacations" a lot, too, for one or two weeks. She always leaves the house a few days after talking with my parents.

Is she going to collect the money?

Why does she leave for so many days?

When she leaves, I am left alone with her son.

He abuses me.

It's horrible.

*****

One day, we're at home: my aunt, her son, and I. But something happens and we need to leave the house. At this moment, I decide to escape. I run six miles as fast as I can to my great aunt's house, my mother's aunt.

I am six years old.

Chapter 4

I arrive at the door. I'm tired and dirty. I'm also really worried. My other aunt and her son are looking for me.

I knock on the door of the house. My mother's aunt opens the door and says, "Andrés, why are you here?"

I enter the house and explain the situation.

"*Tía*, I was abused in the other house. They hit me. They told me I was horrible and that I was never going to see my mom again.

My aunt hugs me and gives me a soda.

 "Calm down, Andrés. Everything is going to be alright."

I sleep for a few hours and then the phone rings. It's a miracle. My mom is calling from the United States. For the first time in a long time, we talk.

"*Mami*[3], I want to see you. I love you and I miss you."

*****

My mom talks with her aunt for a long time. They make a plan. I will travel to the United States with my other aunt, my mother's younger sister.

"Andrés, you need to listen to me. You need to do everything I tell you," my mother says.

During this conversation, my mother explains to me that I am going to travel to see her. I am going to walk through Mexico with her sister to get to the United States.

"But Andrés. Listen. If there's a problem with the officials, you need to tell them that you're going to the United States to visit Disneyland. You need to tell them that you want to see Mickey Mouse, Minnie Mouse, and Donald Duck."

"Okay, *mami*. Why?"

---

[3] Mami: mommy.

My mother explains to me that the officials will be nicer to an innocent child.

In two weeks, my aunt and I will begin our journey.

I am only six years old, and I am leaving my country of Honduras.

THE VOICE

Vol. 7 No. 13   Serrano, Arizona   26 March, 2018

Young Migrants: The Attraction

Sometimes circumstances such as violence and economic problems, push young adults out of their native countries. But there are also attractive reasons that get them to leave their native countries to go somewhere else.

One very important reason is the desire to be with family that is already living in the United States. A lot of the time parents will leave their children in their native countries to go to the "other side." And once they have established themselves in the U.S., and the kids are older, they want to reunite with one another. In fact, a third of the children that cross the border to get to the United States already have at least one parent living in the United States.

Still, another attraction of the journey north is the idea that the laws are less severe for children. For this reason, for young adults that want to escape reality in countries like Honduras, Guatemala and El Salvador, going to the United States is worth the risk.

Chapter 5

The trip through Mexico is really long. My aunt and I walk a lot. We're tired. We don't talk a lot. But when we do talk, I have so many questions because I am still six years old.

I ask, "What's the United States like? Are we really going to Disneyland? Why was I treated badly at the other house?"

My aunt, my mother's younger sister, is 17 years old. She is older than I am, but she doesn't know much.

"The United States is a very big country. There are lots of opportunities there. Someday, yes, we are going to get to Disneyland. Andrés, your other aunt didn't want you. She had problems. Don't worry about it."

It's hard to hear this answer. If they don't want me, will my parents want me?

I ask that question:

"Will my parents want me?"

"Of course, Andrés. Your parents love you with all their hearts. We'll see them soon."
I'm happy. I'm six years old, and I'm going to see my parents.

Scarlett Helmecki, grade 6

Chapter 6

My aunt and I walk a lot. We spend time in different houses in Mexico along the way, with the help of other people.

My aunt explains to me, "Andrés, we are in Mexico illegally. We don't have permission to be in the country."

"Is that why you're nervous?" I ask.

"Yes, Andrés. We need to get to the border in a week. A guide will be waiting for us to help us cross the border."

We walk for four days. We're tired. One day, we get to a *gringo's*[4] house where we spend two nights. The *coyote*[5], in other words, the guide, arrives early to take the group to the border.

At the house we talk with a girl from Guatemala. She's young and is travelling alone.

---

[4] gringo: a Spanish word used to refer to a person from the United States who is not Hispanic or Latino.

[5] coyote: term used in Spanish to refer to a human smuggler.

"Hello," I say to her, "I'm Andrés. What's your name?"

"Hello. I'm Isabel. How old are you, Andrés?"

"I'm six years old. In three months, I'll be seven. And you?"

"I'm 12 years old," she tells me.

"I'm going to the United States to see my mom. Where is your mom?" I ask her.

"My mother is in Nashville. I haven't seen her in a long time," she explains to me.

"I haven't seen my parents either. I really want to see them," I tell her.

Isabel and I talk a lot at the *gringo*'s house. She's really nice.

One night, there's a problem. The police arrive at the house. All the people there are immigrants, including my aunt, Isabel, and me. We need to go to a secret room where we wait for many hours. The situation is serious. Lots of people are yelling. We have to be silent; we can't speak. Then there's another problem: Isabel is not in the room with us. I'm scared. I shouldn't say anything, but I ask my aunt, "Where's Isabel?"

"Shhhhh," she tells me. "Don't talk."

I'm worried. After a long time, I escape from the room to look for my friend. I find her in another part of the house. Something is wrong. There is a lot of blood on her face and on other parts of her body.

"Isabel, what happened to you?" I ask.

"They attacked me," she tells me.

I don't understand much, but I feel bad. I return to the secret room to tell my aunt. I want to help Isabel, but my aunt doesn't let me. She's nervous. Worried. We don't leave the room for many more hours. I don't see my friend Isabel again and I'm sad.

It's difficult to understand the situation because I'm only six years old.

Chapter 7

We continue our journey to the border. My aunt says that we have to cross. I don't know what we need to cross, but I imagine it's something big. All the adults speak of "the border" as something scary and say that the immigration officers are monsters. I don't know what the *migra*[6] is, but I don't like the police or officials.

I'm afraid. But then I think of the other trip: the eventual trip to Disneyland.

We arrive at a motel to spend the night. We're going to cross a river tomorrow. The Río Bravo. It's the river that separates Mexico and the United States.

My aunt says to me, "Andrés, rest. Sleep well. You're going to need a lot of energy tomorrow."

"Okay, *tía*. You, too."

---

[6] migra: informal term to refer to the immigration police or border patrol.

I'm sleeping on the floor when I hear a noise. So many people are yelling again. I don't see anything, but I hear a man's voice:

"Come with us. If you don't, we'll sell the boy to the Zetas."

The men are talking with my aunt. She says to me, "Andrés, don't move."

I don't move. For a long time, I don't move. I don't know where my aunt is, but I don't move.

Finally, my aunt returns to where I am. She is dirty and is crying. There is blood on her mouth.

"*Tía...*" I say.

I want to say more to her, but she doesn't want to talk. She only asks me, "Do you need to use the bathroom? Let's go."

My aunt has taken care of me for a long time. I want to take care of her, too, but I don't know how. I'm only six years old.

Chapter 8

We spend two more days in that house. My aunt doesn't speak. She doesn't say anything. Her eyes are sad. I'm sad too.

I try to talk with her:

"*Tía*, what are you thinking? Are we going to see Donald Duck when we cross the border?"

I am six years old, but I know that we aren't going to see Donald Duck right after we get to the United States. But I want to see my aunt smile. She is not doing well.

My aunt doesn't answer my question, she only says, "Andrés, we're going to cross the river later. You need to prepare yourself. It's really important to pay attention. You need to listen to me."

"Yes, *tía*. I will listen to you."

*****

In the afternoon a man arrives at the house to take us to the river. He's young but he's not nice. I take my aunt's hand and we walk with other people to where the motorboat is. We will use that boat to cross from one side of the river to the other.

The man speaks with us and gives us very important instructions.

"No matter what happens, the goal is to get to the other side to get to the United States. If you fall out of the boat, don't stop. Get to the other side."

We are a small group of five people: four adults and me. We get in the boat. The man guides the boat to the other side. The water in the river is turbulent. Very turbulent. One moment I feel the wind on my face and the next I am in the river.

I don't know what happened. I am scared, but I remember the instructions of the coyote. I take my 6-year-old body and swim to the other side.

Ava Swann, grade 6

Chapter 9

I know how to swim well. Very well. In Quebrada Seca in Honduras, I spent a lot of time in the river with my aunts and other family. I thank God that I can guide my small 6-year-old body to the other side of the river.

The water is very turbulent, and it is difficult for me to swim. I use my arms and legs to help me. I don't see my aunt. I only think about the instructions of the coyote: get to the other side.

I don't know where the boat of the coyote is. I also don't see the people of my group.

There's a lot of noise, too. Many people are screaming: the people in the water and the people on both sides of the river. There are the noises of helicopters, too, but I can't hear them. I hear only the sound of the river. I need to get to the other side.

I don't see anything else on the other side of the river. Finally, I see a part where there aren't many trees. The area is clear. I want to get there. I am concentrating so hard on swimming well that I don't see the men. They are men from the United States Border Patrol.

After an eternity I get to the other side. I'm tired. Exhausted. One of the officers comes over to me.

"Don't move," he tells me.

I look at his face. He is young, thin, and not very tall. He has a hat, but I see he has black hair. He also has a moustache and a beard. He looks like all the men in Mexico. In Honduras, too. Is he a United States officer? He's not a *gringo*, I think.

I don't move. He speaks to me again. "Come with me."

The man speaks Spanish. I understand Spanish, but I don't understand why he's speaking it. I go with the man.

"And my *tía*?" I say to the man, asking where she is.

"We have her somewhere else. Let's go to the station."

When I see my aunt, I hug her tight. We have both walked for days. Weeks. We're tired, but we are alive. She's 17 and I'm 6, and we have finally arrived in the United States.

THE VOICE

Vol. 7 No. 16   Serrano, Arizona   16 April, 2018

Young Migrants: I.C.E.* at the Border

Sometimes children cross by way of the river, and other they cross through the desert. They say that they experience a lot of trauma during the difficult journey, especially seeing many corpses of people that have died along the way.

Immediately after arriving, Mexican children are deported to Mexico again. But when I.C.E. captures Central Americans, they put them in shelters and separate the adults from the children. These shelters are large campuses with schools and sports fields, but they are very similar to prisons because the children can only leave for doctors' and other therapists' appointments.

The majority of these shelters exist in states that border Mexico, in areas away from the cities, but they exist in other states as well. These young adults that arrive alone are almost always invisible in a country as large as the United States.

*I.C.E.: Immigration and Customs Enforcement.

Chapter 10

I am tired from crossing the river and the journey. My aunt is also tired. We walk to the immigration vehicle. The officer says, "Get in. We're going to the station."

My aunt helps me get into the car and we go to the station.

*****

It is sunny and hot, but I'm cold. I'm nervous. And scared. We get out of the car and enter through the front door of the station. We are in the United States. It's a miracle.

I see many people in green and brown uniforms. Many of the people in the station look like the officers that caught me at the river: they are brown skinned with black hair and brown eyes, too. Just like me. Are we really in the United States?

Right then, a woman officer looks at me and speaks.

"Sit down. What's your name?"

"My name is Andrés," I tell her.

"Hello Andrés. How are you?" the officer asks me.

"Good."

I don't want to say much because I'm nervous.

"How old are you, Andrés?" the woman asks me.

"Six years old," I respond.

"What country are you from?"

"I'm from Honduras. My town's name is Quebrada Seca," I tell her.

"And Andrés, where are you going?" the officer asks me.

The question. I have practiced answering this question for many weeks. At that moment, I remember what my mother told me.

"I am going to Disneyland. I am going to see Mickey Mouse and Donald Duck.

I look at the smile on the officer's face. She is nice. Once I gave her this information, I'm not nervous anymore.

"Good, Andrés. We're going to help you because you need to get to Disneyland. Mickey Mouse is waiting for you."

Chapter 11

The officials call my parents. They will come to pick us up, but my aunt and I have to spend a few days in a detention center. In the center there are a lot of people: women, men, and a lot of children. I'm not with my aunt. I am with other kids. Normally I like playing with other children, but I don't play with anyone here. I am counting the moments until I see my mom. I haven't seen her for many years. I've only spoken with her on the telephone.

After three days, an officer comes to the room where I am.

"Come on. They are here to pick you up."

I leave the room. The officer accompanies me to another room where there is the most beautiful sight in the world: my mom. I haven't seen her in almost five years. My heart is filled with so much love. I have so many emotions that I can't respond when she speaks to me.

"Andrés, look at you, *mijo*[7]. I love you so much!"

There are other people in the room. My father is there, my aunt, and many officers from the border patrol, that is, the *migra*. But I am only focused on one thing: my mom. I've dreamed of this day for many years.

Shyly, I walk to where my mom is and hug her. I feel complete.

At six years old, I don't know what to think. The dream from long ago... is now real.

---

[7] mijo: my son.

Chapter 12

My aunt and I spent a few more days at the shelter in Texas. I see my parents every day as they talk a lot with the immigration officials. We need to organize many documents and official papers before returning to Connecticut.

My mom and I talk a lot. For four years I have only spoken to her on the phone. I have had so many dreams about my mother and now I am finally with her.

"Andrés, tomorrow we are going to Connecticut by car."

"Ok, *mami*. What is Conn-ect...?" It is impossible to pronounce this word.

"Conn-EC-ticut. It is a state in the United States. It is where we live. We live in a town called..."

I interrupt my mom with a question. Now that I am with my parents, I have many questions.

"*Mami*, are we ever going to go back to Quebrada Seca?"

"No, *mijo*. We don't live there anymore. We live here in the United States."

"*Mami*, are we going to be in a new house tomorrow?"

"We will be going to the house. We are going to be in the car for a few days. Connecticut is far from here."

I have a lot of questions, but the conversation ends when my dad enters the room. He talks with us.

"Rosalinda told me that we can leave tomorrow. We have all the documents. We need to speak with an attorney when we get back to Connecticut."

I don't understand the conversation. And I also don't understand the other conversations with the officers because they speak English. I don't know English. I know a few words like "hello" and "thank you," but I can't speak. It's difficult.

My father says, "Andrés, come here."

My father gives me a hug and asks me, "Are you ready to go to the new house?"

I don't know my father. I have not seen him for a long time. I don't know what to say to him. I am very happy to be with my mother, but I'm also very nervous.

I answer with only one word: Yes.

But is that true? Am I ready?

THE VOICE

Vol. 7 No. 20   Serrano, Arizona   7 May, 2018

Young Migrants: The U.S. Government

The number of young children that arrive in the United States presents a big problem for the federal government. There are no adequate resources that can maintain all these new people. In the shelters, the children must be fed and educated, and they must also find the children's families in the country. But it's also necessary to find out if the families of the children aren't using the children for other reasons, like human trafficking.

It is good for the children that the federal government can't deport them without having a court hearing (to prevent human trafficking), but it is bad for the United States because there is not enough money to provide good service for the children.

Chapter 13

In the car to Connecticut, I see so much: many other cars, enormous stores, and vehicles in the sky. But I don't know what they're called.

"*Mami*, what are those?" I ask looking at the sky.

"Those are airplanes."

"Airplanes?" I ask. I still don't understand. I have never seen "airplanes" in my six years of living (though I will be seven soon.)

"Airplanes are like buses in the sky. They transport people."

I'm fascinated. For the rest of the trip, I look out the window of the car, looking for airplanes.

*****

After another long trip in the car, we arrive in Connecticut. And I still can't pronounce this word well.

I am in the apartment one day when my mom tells me, "Andrés, tomorrow you are going to go to school."

I think of the school in Quebrada Seca. I liked school and I liked my teacher.

"Great, *mami*. I like school."

*****

The new school is not like my school in Quebrada Seca. It's very different. Yes, there are many students, but there are only two students like me. Their names are Carlos and Catalina. I talk a lot with them because they speak Spanish. The other students speak English. I don't know English. English is difficult.

I go to class every day. I try to understand. Numbers are easy and I learn them well. But when we read and practice words, I am very frustrated. I can't read. The teacher helps me, or tries to help me, but she can't speak Spanish.

She tells me, "House. This word is house."

On the paper I see a photo of a house with the word "house" next to it. I say, "*Casa. Es una casa[8].*"

"House," she repeats.

I already know how to read in Spanish, and I read well. I read and pronounce the word "O-u-se" but the teacher repeats "hOU-s." All the other children in the class work, read, and draw. I can't. The class frustrates me a lot.

One day in the afternoon I arrive home in a bad mood.

"Good afternoon," my mom says.

I don't say anything to my mom, my favorite person in the world. I walk directly to my room and start crying. I cry a lot. I am very frustrated.

My mom is a very calm person. After a few minutes she walks into my room and speaks to me with love. "Andrés, are you ok? What happened?"

---

[8] Casa. Es una casa: House. It's a house.

I don't want to talk to my mom. I don't want to talk to anybody. I don't want to go back to school. I don't want to be in the United States. I don't want to stay here with my family. I want to be in Honduras. I want to speak Spanish. I want to be with my friends in my school. I want...

"Andrés?" She sits on the bed. She touches my head and asks again, "What's wrong?"

After crying for a few more minutes, I explain everything that happened at school that day. I tell her that it's very difficult, that I don't like it, and that I don't want to go back.

My mom listens to me. When I finish talking, she tells me, "Andrés, you're very smart. You're also very creative, nice, and diligent."

"Diligent? What's that?" I ask.

"You know how to work. You have the determination to do what you want to in life.

"But mom.... English is so hard."

"*Mijo*, everything is hard in life at first. If you want to read in English, you're going to read in English. You have to study, but you can do it."

My mom asks for a hug, and I give one to her. I love my mom, and she loves me.

*****

The next day I go to school with new determination: I am going to read in English, and I am going to speak it too.

At the end of the school year, after I've been in the United States for eight months, I read and speak English very well. I am seven years old.

Chapter 14

The years pass. I live happily with my family: my parents and my little brother. My brother was born in the United States. So, he's American.

During the first few years I study a lot at school and at home. I always do my homework in the kitchen while my mom makes dinner.

One day while she's preparing roast beef we have a talk. I'm in fifth grade and am doing science homework on natural disasters: tornados, hurricanes, and earthquakes.

"Mom, do you know about natural disasters?"

"Yes, Andrés. Sure. Why are you asking?" my mom asks me.

"We're studying them in science class," I tell her. "What do you know about them?"

We live in a part of the United States that does not have a very severe climate. Yes, there are four seasons, and it is very hot in the summer and very cold (with snow!) in the winter. But for the most part, it doesn't cause problems.

"Son, it is because of a hurricane that we are here in the United States," my mom explains to me.

"How?"

While my mom continues preparing the food, she explains about Hurricane Mitch, which hit Honduras when I was only a year old, causing my parents to leave Honduras.

THE VOICE

Vol. 7 No. 21   Serrano, Arizona   21 May, 2018

Because of the Storm: Hurricane Mitch

In October of 1998, Hurricane Mitch made landfall. The tragic storm brought 25 inches of rain that caused mass destruction in many countries in Central America. Ten thousand people died and almost three million were left without homes.

It destroyed the infrastructure and the economy of these countries. People were left without homes and jobs, and these countries did not have the resources necessary to help the people. With the serious situation in Honduras and Nicaragua, many media reports in the United States gave Temporary Protection Status (TPS) to those affected. Many people began to leave their countries, looking for work in other places to make money for their families.

Chapter 15

For many years everything goes well for me and my family. I almost forget the abuse and torturous experiences in Honduras during that horrible time of my life. I'm content and happy.

I attend school and enter a special program for smart kids in the city. I'm a good student. I impress my teachers a lot. I participate in many contests and win lots of prizes. In the first year of high school, I win first place at a science fair. First place in the entire state! I'm very happy when they tell me. The principal calls me to her office to speak with me.

"Congratulations, Andrés. I was told that you won first place in the entire state for your science experiment."

"Thank you. What did I win?" I ask her.

"It is a scholarship of ten thousand dollars to a private university in the state," she tells me.

"Wow! That's great! Thank you!"

I don't know what to think. Ten thousand dollars! That's a lot of money! And for college. I talk with my parents a lot about college and how I want to go. They support my dreams and would love to help me, but the truth is that college costs a lot of money. And this is not the only problem.

*****

One day I speak with my mom.

"Andrés," she says to me. "I don't know if you can attend the university. We don't have the money."

"But, with the prize money..." I say. "And I can take loans to attend college."

"Andrés, no. I spoke with a woman at the bank, and she told me that it's not possible. You're not a citizen of this country."

I'm very frustrated. "What? I can't go to college because I wasn't born here?"

"It's not like that. Yes, you can attend without the official documents, but you have to have the money to pay for it because there's no financial aid for the undocumented."

"Not even for the DREAMers?" I ask my mom.

I'm referring to the DREAM Act (Development, Relief, and Education for Alien Minors Act) where the US government gives certain young people the opportunity to attend college.

"Mom, why do I study so much in high school and take hard classes if I'm not going to continue studying in college?"

"Andrés, calm down. Don't get angry. We'll find a solution."

Normally my mom calms me with her love. Those instinctive acts she has done for me so far in my life have helped me a lot. My mom loves me a lot, that's true. And I love her, too, but today, I'm furious.

Chapter 16

I continue this struggle daily, the struggle of my studies and the struggle of being undocumented. It's been ten years, a whole decade since I came to the United States.

I finally make it to the last year of high school. Like all the other years, I'm taking difficult classes. This semester I'm in advanced calculus (AP). I study a lot. I like math and know a lot, but my test grades are bad, and I don't understand why. I talk with one of my classmates.

"Hey, Charlie. What answer did you get for number 12? And number 23?" I ask him.

Charlie tells me his answers and shows me his test. I have the same answers as he does, but the teacher marked mine wrong. When I ask my teacher about my test, her answer surprises me. It also makes me angry.

"You're lucky to be in this class. You should be grateful for the opportunity to learn with the other students."

Although she doesn't say it, I understand what she means: I'm undocumented, and she thinks I don't deserve to be in the class.

*****

This incident happens at the beginning of the school year and affects me a lot. Another thing that affects me is seeing my friends apply to college.

The questions are the same every day:

"Andrés, how many colleges are you applying to?"

"Andrés, do you want help applying?"

It's a rite that happens all over the United States, but it's one that I can't participate in. I respond with vague answers and fake smiles.

I feel sad. All the work I've done so far, and for what?

I feel depressed.

I start to skip school.

I just don't go.

I can't get out of bed.

I feel really bad.

What's happening to me?

THE VOICE

Vol. 7 No. 23   Serrano, Arizona   4 June, 2018

Young Migrants:
The Education System

The education system, like the federal government in the United States, does not have many resources for all the children and young adults that come to the country first and then attend the schools. Here in the United States, it's the law that all children must attend school.

These young adults that arrive have scars of poverty or violence, or both. Additionally, the children arrive constantly during the school year. Schools must offer many services and support with courses that teach English: ESL, psychologists, and bilingual professionals. But like with any emotional issue, there are people that think that we should not spend resources and tax dollars for educating those that came to the United States illegally.

Chapter 17

For months I can hardly function. I miss so many days of school that I get expelled. I don't do anything. Nothing. Life goes on — mine, too — but I can't participate in it. It's depression. I'm in a bad way. Although I don't want to die or harm myself, I also don't want to live. I don't know what to do.

My mom knows what's going on. Mothers always know.

"Andrés, get up. It's time to go to the doctor. A lady at work gave me the name and number of a psychologist that can help you."

I don't want to, but I don't have any reason not to go, so I get up and get ready to visit the doctor.

The session with Dr. Rosado goes very well. He gives me a chance to talk about myself after asking me a few basic questions. I talk about the problems I'm having with high school, with my friends, and with my math teacher. I don't want to talk at first, but once

I start, I can't stop. I tell him everything that has happened to me in my life.

Dr. Rosado listens to me without saying much. I feel very comfortable talking to him because he doesn't stop me from talking. He listens to everything I say. I feel relieved. The stress goes away a little. For the first time in months, I feel human again.

We make plans for more sessions, once a week. Although I'm not happy, I feel better. The view is clearing.

*****

My dad comes home that night and I tell him about my appointment with Dr. Rosado. My dad always comes home tired because he's starting his own business in the city. His company is due to open in two days. Every day my dad goes to work at a local restaurant where he cooks all day, and at night he does the necessary work to open his own business. My dad works hard.

"Hi, *papá*[9]. How was your day?" I ask him.
_____
[9] papá: dad.

My dad looks at me with surprise. This is the first time I've greeted him in a long time and the change is noticeable. He greets me, too.

"How are you, Andrés? I'm happy to see you today. Did something happen?" my father asks.

Normally when we talk, it's about superficial matters. We're not used to talking about the problems in our lives, but I know that he cares about me.

"Today I went to talk with a therapist. It went well. We talked a lot. I feel much better," I say to him.

My dad is very traditional, and a bit closed off. He is not a cold person, but I know that he is suspicious of doctors in general, so I don't know how he'll receive the news.

But he notices that I'm talking to him, and that I want to talk more, so he continues the conversation.

"That's good, Andrés. That's very good for you."

"Dad, you've asked me many times before but... can I help with your business?"

Now my father understands why my mom made the appointment. With the idea that I can leave my problems and stresses with my therapist, I can continue living again. And my father is happy.

"Yes, *hijo*[10]. I would love for you to work with me."

And, uncharacteristically, he hugs me tight.

---

[10] hijo: son.

Chapter 18

Another year passes. I have sessions with Dr. Rosado every week and I work with my father. Every day we go to the building where the business will be to do the necessary construction work, as well as make other plans. I don't have as severe depression as I did before, but every day I think of college and the high school diploma that I didn't earn.

I'm working one day when I receive a text from a school counselor. It says:

> My name is Mr. Archer. How are you? I've been told that you're working. Call me please. We need to talk."

Immediately, I have so many questions.

What does he want? Why is he contacting me now? Why has he not contacted me before?

I keep my phone in my pants pocket and continue working. Today I'm in charge of setting up all the technology for the business.

I like technology and I read a lot of books about code.

After working for four hours, I take out my phone and call the counselor.

"Hello, Mr. Archer. This is Andrés Lopez. Did you contact me?

"Yes, Andrés. How have you been? I think about you a lot."

"Thank you, sir."

We talk a little about my life now and what happened in the months after I left high school.

"Andrés, do you still want to attend college someday? I want you to think about finishing your studies so you can get your high school diploma."

"Sir, you know I want to continue studying. I love learning. But without official documents, I can't apply for scholarships or loans."

"I understand. But, step by step, right? You won't be able to do anything without a high school diploma. What do you think about starting there?"

"Sir, I work every day. I have two jobs. I can't quit them to attend high school."

"Because of that I want you to finish your studies online. You can do the work when you can."

And with this conversation I start to finish my studies to get a high school diploma: the first step.

*****

I don't know what will happen in the future. The DACA status I have to be able to work will expire in a few months and the legal situation may change. I want to follow the laws of the country, but I also want to continue working. Ever since I arrived in the country, I wanted to go to college, and for this I need money. It's difficult to be in a situation that is in limbo, especially while also being undocumented.

Sometimes my experiences cause me a lot of problems mentally and emotionally, but I keep them in mind and how they have contributed to my life: the trauma and the joy. And I know I need to keep going.

So, I do.

Ghost Moon Lullaby
by: Jennifer Lighty

The children facing the cameras
don't complain. They're not fooled by concrete or
the lack of windows.
They know that borders mean nothing to ghosts
and that if they fall asleep under the moon
they'll wake up under a sun that will burn
the skin right off their flesh
leaving them with nothing but bones
not even a mother could recognize.
The guards don't understand
why they don't try to escape.

Jennifer Lighty is a writer, teacher, and mentor
whose work aims to bridge the gap between
imagination and logic through myth, traditional
oral stories, and poetry. Author of three books of
poetry, *Siren, Bluebell: The Apocalypse Diary*
and *Breaking Up With the Moon* (Finishing Line
Press, 2017), her poems and essays have
appeared in numerous publications including
Earthlines, the *Island Review*, *Poetry Lore*, *The
North American Review*, *The Providence
Journal*, and *Thrush Poetry Journal*. Her poem,
"That Which There Are No Words For" was
nominated for the Pushcart Prize. Jennifer also

received a fellowship grant in poetry from the Rhode Island State Council on the Arts. *Piko: A Return to the Dreaming*, her nonfiction account of a 21-day ceremony enacted on Hawai'i Island telling stories to a body of water will be published by Whale Road Press in 2023. She writes weekly on the intersection of myth, ecology, current events, and daily life at The Corpus Callosum Chronicles. For more information on Jennifer's multidimensional work, please visit www.aquaodyssey.com.

https://jenlighty.substack.com/

ABOUT THE AUTHOR

Jennifer Degenhardt taught high school Spanish for over 20 years and now teaches at the college level. At the time she realized her own high school students, many of whom had learning challenges, acquired language best through stories, so she began to write ones that she thought would appeal to them. She has been writing ever since.

Other titles by Jen Degenhardt:

La chica nueva | *La Nouvelle Fille* | The New Girl | *Das Neue Mädchen* | *La nuova ragazza*
La chica nueva (the ancillary/workbook volume, Kindle book, audiobook)
Salida 8 | *Sortie no. 8*
Chuchotenango | *La terre des chiens errants* | *La vita dei cani*
Pesas | *Poids et haltères* | Weights and Dumbbells |*Pesi*
Luis, un soñador

65

El jersey | <u>The Jersey</u> | *Le maillot*
La mochila | <u>The Backpack</u> | *Le sac à dos*
Moviendo montañas | *Déplacer les montagnes* | <u>Moving Mountains</u> | *Spostando montagne*
La vida es complicada | *La vie est compliquée* | <u>Life is Complicated</u>
La vida es complicada Practice & Questions (workbook)
El Mundial | *La Coupe du Monde* | <u>The World Cup</u>
Quince | <u>Fifteen</u> | *Douze ans*
Quince Practice & Questions (workbook)
El viaje difícil | *Un voyage difficile* | <u>A Difficult Journey</u>
La niñera
¡¿Fútbol...americano?! | *Football...américain ?!*
Era una chica nueva
Levantando pesas: un cuento en el pasado
Se movieron las montañas
Fue un viaje difícil
¿Qué pasó con el jersey?
Cuando se perdió la mochila
Con (un poco de) ayuda de mis amigos | <u>With (a little) Help from My Friends</u> | *Un petit coup de main amical*
La última prueba | <u>The Last Test</u>
Los tres amigos | <u>Three Friends</u> | *Drei Freunde* | *Les trois amis*
La evolución musical
María María: un cuento de un huracán | <u>María María: A Story of a Storm</u> | *Maria Maria: un histoire d'un orage*
Debido a la tormenta | <u>Because of the Storm</u>
La lucha de la vida | <u>The Fight of His Life</u>
Secretos | *Secrets*
Como vuela la pelota
Cambios | *Changements* | <u>Changes</u>
El pueblo | <u>The Town</u>

66

@JenniferDegenh1

@jendegenhardt9

@PuentesLanguage &
World LanguageTeaching Stories (group)

Visit www.puenteslanguage.com to sign up to receive
information on new releases and other events.

Check out all titles as ebooks with audio on
www.digilangua.co.

ABOUT THE COVER ARTISTS

Elysees Lincecum is a high school student in Southern California, who has been drawing for as long as she can remember. Along with art, she is passionate about reading and music. Elysees enjoys reading, drawing, and hanging out with her friends and family. During the summer, she spends time traveling and hanging out with her family from Texas and Colorado. Follow Elysees on Instagram to see more of her art at @artbyetl.

Dante Hall is an artist and aspiring filmmaker with an interest in horror and science-fiction. He developed a love for art as soon as he could hold a pencil. Drawing, painting, and graphic art are among his strengths. Dante has designed activity books, written short stories and screenplays, and designed no-content journals. Dante is also the illustrator of the book, *Two Homes*.

Dante enjoys spending time with his brother and his friends, creating videos for his YouTube channel, Fun with Dante, and working on new skills at his parkour gym. Dante loves learning new languages and about different cultures.

www.ingramcontent.com/pod-product-compliance
Lightning Source LLC
Chambersburg PA
CBHW060349050426
42449CB00011B/2887